HAWKS

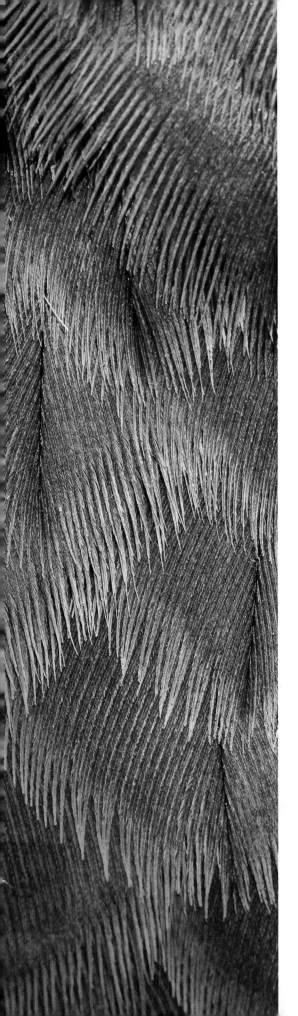

LIVING WILD

Published by Creative Education
P.O. Box 227, Mankato, Minnesota 56002
Creative Education is an imprint of The Creative Company
www.thecreativecompany.us

Design and production by Mary Herrmann
Art direction by Rita Marshall
Printed in the United States of America

Photographs by Alamy (Greg Balfour Evans, FLPA), Dreamstime (Baloo2, Boykov, Linda Bucklin, Martine De Graaf, Melinda Fawver, Donald Fink, Hdcphoto, Hugocorzo, Jakich, Rck953, Roim, Ginger Sanders), iStockphoto (Edoma), PeregrineFund.org, Shutterstock (B & T Media Group Inc., Thomas Barrat, Maxim Blinkov, Steve Byland, cowboy54, Brendon Cremer, Kjersti Joergensen, Narisa Koryanyong, Dennis Ku, Rob McKay, Pavel Mikoska, Tyler Miller, Michal Ninger, Randimal, Ruta Production, skn, Mike Truchon, Vishnevskiy Vasily, waysidelynne), SuperStock (Minden Pictures), Wikipedia (Kanalu Chock, cuatrok77, DickDaniels, Haukurth, JonRichfield, Kuroyasha, Mike Morel, Alastair Rae, Dominic Sherony, Jan Willem Steffelaar, Alan Vernon, Henry Walters)

Library of Congress Cataloging-in-Publication Data
Gish, Melissa.
Hawks / Melissa Gish.
p. cm. — (Living wild)
Includes bibliographical references and index.
Summary: A scientific look at hawks, including their habitats, physical characteristics such as their wings, behaviors, relationships with humans, and variety of the hunting raptors in the world today.
ISBN 978-1-60818-418-7
1. Hawks—Juvenile literature. I. Title. II. Series: Living wild.

QL696.F32G573 2014
598.9'44—dc23   2013031811

CCSS: RI.5.1, 2, 3, 8; RST.6-8.1, 2, 5, 6, 8; RH.6-8.3, 4, 5, 6, 7, 8

First Edition
9 8 7 6 5 4 3 2 1

CREATIVE EDUCATION

HAWKS

Melissa Gish

On the Philippine island of Polillo, a warm wind gusts through a rice paddy. High above, a Polillo crested

goshawk circles, taking in every movement below.

On the Philippine island of Polillo, a warm wind gusts through a rice paddy, sending a mass of dragonflies into the air like wisps of blue and silver string. High above, a Polillo crested goshawk circles, taking in every movement below. The bird flaps its wings twice and then floats, drifting effortlessly like a kite. Tilting one wing, the goshawk makes a turn in the opposite direction and begins to descend.

The dancing dragonflies have drawn the attention of forest frogs, which leap out of the rice paddy to capture the bouncing insects. But the hunters become the hunted. The goshawk tucks its wings and dives toward the earth, its eyes trained on a plump frog. Before the frog realizes it is in danger, the goshawk skims the ground feet-first, drives its sharp talons into the frog's soft flesh, and lifts the creature into the air.

WHERE IN THE WORLD THEY LIVE

■ **Short-tailed Hawk**
southern Florida,
Mexico to south-
eastern Brazil

■ **Common Buzzard**
Europe, Eurasia,
Japan

■ **Red-tailed Hawk**
North and Central
America

■ **Sharp-shinned
Hawk**
North America

■ **Ferruginous Hawk**
North American
grasslands

■ **African Goshawk**
central and
southern Africa

■ **Black
Sparrowhawk**
sub-Saharan Africa

■ **Shikra**
Asian and African
forests

The nearly 100 species of hawks are found in wild
populations throughout the world, from Australia to
North America. The birds known as true hawks make up
the greatest number of the hawk family, but the buteos
are the most widely distributed and include many
birds called "buzzards." The colored squares represent
habitats of select species from each group.

SHARP AS A HAWK

ike all birds, hawks are **warm-blooded**, feathered, beaked animals that walk on two feet and lay eggs. Like their ancestors, all modern birds have hollow bones, making them lightweight for flight. Hawks belong to a group of birds called raptors. Female hawks are up to one-third larger than males, a characteristic that is common among raptors. They feed on a variety of small prey, from insects and worms to ground squirrels, snakes, and other birds. If they are very hungry, hawks will even eat **carrion**. The largest hawk, the ferruginous hawk of North America, grows to only about five pounds (2.3 kg) yet may kill prey slightly larger than itself, such as jackrabbits that weigh six pounds (2.7 kg). The sharp-shinned hawk, also of North America, is the continent's smallest hawk, with females weighing less than eight ounces (227 g).

Hawks are members of the family Accipitridae, which also includes eagles, vultures, and other birds of prey. The name "Accipiter" (*AK-sip-it-ER*) comes from the Latin *accipere*, which means "to take or seize" and refers to the way these birds attack their prey. The *Buteo* genus

Zone-tailed hawks resemble turkey vultures and often fly with them to trick prey, since vultures do not hunt live animals.

The endangered Puerto Rican sharp-shinned hawk feeds almost exclusively on hummingbirds and small songbirds.

of the Accipitridae family includes 38 birds that are called buzzards in Europe but broad-winged hawks in North America, and the subfamily Accipitrinae includes 56 birds that are known worldwide as short-winged hawks or "true" hawks. The difference in wing structure, which determines hunting and feeding behaviors, is what distinguishes the two groups of hawks.

Buteos, which have long wings and short tails, are known as soaring hawks. In open spaces, these hawks ride upward-moving currents of warm air. These circular currents are called thermals. By riding thermals, soaring hawks are able to hang almost motionless for hours, rarely flapping their wings. As they drift along, they search for prey below. Their bodies are heavy, and they drop on their prey like rocks, crushing bone and using their powerful feet and long talons to puncture soft flesh and organs. True hawks, which have short wings and long tails, are known as forest hawks. They do not soar. Rather, they perch and watch for prey to approach. Once they spot a potential meal, these hawks burst downward, flapping their wings furiously. They can maneuver quickly, whipping around trees and other obstacles with

The ability to tightly curve or turn in their wings gives "true" hawks great maneuvering power.

coming for that

The broad wings of a buteo, or soaring hawk, allow it to quietly drop down on prey as if wearing a parachute.

ease. When they land on their prey, they repetitively drive their talons into the animal's body to kill it.

Hawks develop their hunting skills when they are young by practicing attacking and "killing" non-animal objects. Hawks have been observed grabbing and shredding corncobs and pine cones. After tearing these objects to pieces with their strong beaks and sharp talons, the birds do not eat the cobs or pine cones. **Ornithologists** believe such behavior helps hawks improve their speed and footwork in attacking and killing prey. Hawks have three toes that point forward and one that points backward. The middle toe in front and the back toe are the shortest, but they have the longest talons. The beak and talons are made of keratin, the same material found in human fingernails, and grow throughout a hawk's life. Clawing on the bones of prey and clutching tree branches and other perches keep hawk talons from growing too long.

Birds have no teeth, but their sharp beaks can rip and crush flesh. Grinding the beak against bones while feeding keeps it both sharp and worn down to an appropriate length. When eating something that cannot be swallowed

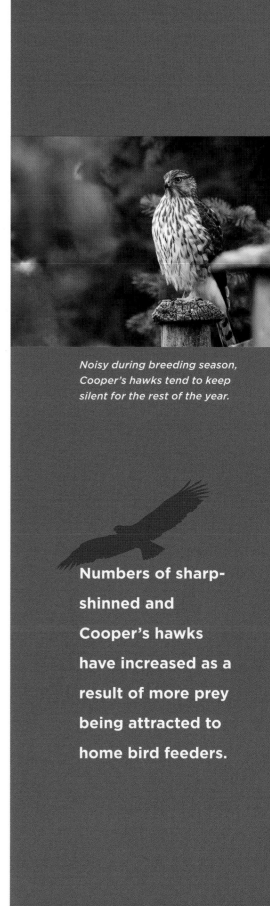

Noisy during breeding season, Cooper's hawks tend to keep silent for the rest of the year.

Numbers of sharp-shinned and Cooper's hawks have increased as a result of more prey being attracted to home bird feeders.

For most hawks, only about one in every four attacks results in the successful capture of a meal.

whole, a hawk uses its hooked beak to rip into prey, tearing flesh to pieces. Then, using the edges of its beak like knives, the hawk slices off bite-sized pieces. Hawks eat 15 to 50 percent of their body weight in food each day. Studies have determined that hawks are intelligent birds, and they plan ahead. When food is plentiful, hawks gorge themselves, filling their crop with food until it is swollen, in case their next meal is some days away.

Among warm-blooded animals, only birds have a crop, which is located at the base of the neck. The crop stores food and allows only small portions at a time to move into the two-part stomach. The first part of the stomach, called the proventriculus (*proh-ven-TRIK-yuh-lus*), contains digestive juices that break down food. The material then passes to the ventriculus, or gizzard. Birds regularly eat gravel or grit, which settles in the muscular gizzard and is used to grind solids into liquid mush. Having an efficient digestion system is especially important for raptors, which often devour bones. Birds have a high **metabolism** and digest food over a prolonged period, which is why birds defecate often—from 25 to 50 times per day.

Short-tailed hawks in Florida are darker in color than those that reside in Central and South America.

With little time to hunt at dusk, bat hawks have been observed devouring as many as 11 bats within an 18-minute span.

Most hawks are active during the day, though some hawks hunt at dawn and dusk. The bat hawk, found in Africa and southern Asia, is named for its diet. A true hawk, the bat hawk flies at high speeds, maneuvering with deep swoops and sharp turns, to chase down bats, which it hunts at dusk, when these prey first emerge for their nighttime activity. Unlike their distant relatives the owls, hawks are not nocturnal (active at night). In fact, several unusual species of owl are called hawk owls because they are daytime hunters like hawks.

Hawks have acute hearing and powerful vision. A hawk's eye has a nictitating (*NIK-tih-tate-ing*) membrane (a see-through inner eyelid) that closes from front to back, wiping dust from the eyeball and shielding the sensitive **pupil** from direct sunlight. To locate food, hawks rely on what is called binocular vision. A hawk's eyes are located on the sides of its skull but face forward, so hawks can look outward and forward at the same time. This binocular vision helps hawks judge distances precisely. Hawks can also focus on objects that are far away. Their vision is eight times more powerful than the sharpest human vision; in fact, raptors have the sharpest distance vision of any animal on Earth.

The two-inch-long (5.1 cm) tarantula hawk wasp is named for its ferocious hunting of tarantulas, which it feeds to its offspring.

While diving toward prey on the ground, red-tailed hawks may travel as fast as 120 miles (193 km) per hour.

SKY DANCERS

Many large hawks, such as red-tailed hawks, can live up to 21 years in the wild or almost 30 years in captivity. Smaller hawks, such as Harris's hawks, typically live no more than 12 years. Hawks reach maturity and are ready to mate at two years of age. Most hawk species remain with a single mate for a breeding season but do not mate for life. Some species, such as red-tailed and Cooper's hawks and the African goshawk, typically mate for life—or until one of the pair dies.

Breeding times for hawks vary among species, with mate selection taking place from January to April in North America and from July to November in Africa, Asia, and Australia. Hawks look for a mate that will be a good provider for their young. Strong flight skills are an indication of a hawk's ability to capture prey for its offspring, so aerial acrobatics called flight displays are part of hawks' courtship. In one such display, a hawk flies high into the sky, folds its wings, and then plunges downward at high speed. At the last moment, the hawk swoops upward to avoid hitting the ground. This up-and-down movement may be repeated up to six times in

The Chinese sparrowhawk travels from the forests of Siberia and China to the Philippines to feed on frogs and lizards.

Harris's hawks typically hunt in pairs or trios, taking turns flushing out prey, chasing it, and attacking it.

swift succession. In another display, a pair of hawks flies high into the air and locks talons. Then together they fall, spinning cartwheels in the air. The two break apart at the last moment and fly back up into the sky. Some male hawks also fly directly at a prospective mate and transfer prey from his talons to hers while in flight. That display is commonly called sky dancing.

Not all courtship displays take place in the air. Sometimes hawks rub their beaks together, bob their heads, and bow to one another in a show of submission— behaviors that establish a bond. Once hawks impress each other and begin to bond, they solidify their relationship through nest building. Hawk nests, called aeries, are always built high above the ground in trees, on ledges or cliffs, or in buildings. Both hawk partners contribute to the nest, which is usually made of sticks and branches the birds have ripped from trees and then lined with bark and fresh greenery. Rarely do hawks pick up nest materials from the ground. Some hawk species reuse their nests year after year, while others make new nests—sometimes multiple times—each year. Nests can be as large as three feet (0.9 m) across.

Like all hawks, western marsh-harriers, which mate from March to May, participate in courtship displays.

Most female hawks lay one to three eggs (though some species lay up to seven) at a rate of one egg per day. A group of eggs is called a clutch. If the eggs are destroyed, as sometimes happens when nests are raided by predators or blown down by wind, most hawks will lay a second or even third clutch. The eggs are two to five inches (5.1– 12.7 cm) long, depending on the species, and vary in color from dull white to tan, brown, or dark-spotted brown.

Like all birds' eggs, hawk eggs must be incubated, or kept warm, while the baby hawks are developing inside. In most species, both parents participate in the task of incubation, though females spend the most time on the nest. A female hawk gently sits with the eggs situated under her breast and wings, and the male brings food to her. Depending on the species, hawks incubate their eggs from 21 to 35 days, after which time the baby hawks, called hatchlings, emerge.

Using its **egg tooth**, the hatchling chips through the hard shell of its egg. At first, the hatchling is covered with white down, but these fluffy feathers soon grow darker and thicker. In most hawk species, feathers begin to replace the down after just a few weeks. By six weeks of age, a baby hawk, now called a fledgling, has feathers and learns to use its wings. As it gains strength, a fledgling may leave the nest to explore its surroundings, but it will depend on its parents to feed it for several more weeks.

At two to three months of age, the young hawk is a juvenile, flying everywhere with its parents to learn how to hunt. The first year of a hawk's life is the most perilous. It must develop its hunting skills, avoid being killed by larger hawks, and find a place to live that is not already inhabited by other, territorial hawks. Some hawks **migrate** annually, like the Swainson's hawk, which travels 7,000 miles (11,265 km) from North America to Argentina each winter. Young

Often, one parent will stand guard and defend the nest as the other parent hunts for food to give the chicks.

The last remaining hawk species native to Hawaii, the endangered Hawaiian hawk breeds only on Hawaii's Big Island.

Habitat destruction pushes many hawk species into ever shrinking breeding and hunting territories.

From Mexico throughout Central and most of South America, the roadside hawk preys on small monkeys.

hawks of migrating species face the added challenges of navigating migration routes while still honing their hunting skills and learning how to avoid predators. Only about half of all hatchlings survive to adulthood. Among red-tailed hawks, the number is even smaller.

An adult hawk's only natural enemies are larger raptors. While hawks provide a useful service to humans in the form of rodent control, hawks often suffer negative effects of human activity. Urban development, agriculture, and logging can disturb nesting sites and destroy habitat. Also, many hawks sit on poles, fence posts, and signs near roadways. Because hawks must drop to the ground to capture prey, one of the greatest threats they face is collision with vehicles. Hawks will fly into the path of a moving vehicle without even seeing the vehicle because a hunting hawk sees only the prey on which its eyes are fixed.

Like most birds, hawks are legally protected from hunting under the United States Migratory Bird Treaty Act and rules established by CITES, an international treaty created in 1973 to protect wildlife from overuse and unsafe trade. Nevertheless, hawks around the world fall victim to **poachers** for their feathers and organs,

which are believed by some people to have medicinal or magical properties. In addition to poaching, destroying hawk habitat and harassing hawks are practices that have reduced the numbers of many hawk species and driven several—including the grey-backed hawk, which may have fewer than 1,000 individuals remaining in scattered parts of Ecuador and Peru—to the brink of **extinction**.

Red-tailed hawks are the most common large hawks in both urban and rural areas of North America.

A statue of Horus was carved at the Temple of Edfu, the second-largest temple in Egypt, between 237 and 57 B.C.

PROTECTION AND PERFORMANCE

The mythological Yggdrasil is home to or provides food for several creatures in addition to the birds.

In **cultures** around the world, hawks are symbols of courage and wisdom, so they are also associated with many stories of heroism. From the ancient Greeks to the North American Indians and First Peoples, people thought of hawks as spiritual messengers between the gods and humans. Seeing a hawk was considered to be an omen, or a symbolic message. In the Lakota Indian tradition, it meant that something important would soon happen. In ancient Celtic tradition, seeing a hawk meant that a person should pursue some creative activity or embark on a quest.

Hawks were often associated with special powers. The Egyptian god Horus is depicted as having a human body and the head of a falcon, a hawk relative. Horus had the power to see into the future. As symbols of the soul, falcons and hawks in ancient Egypt were considered royal birds. In Norse **mythology**, Veðrfölnir is a hawk representing courage that sits on the forehead of Vidofnir the eagle and directs Vidofnir's judgment. The birds are perched in a tree called Yggdrasil, which represents the connections between the people, their gods, the giants, and the dead—all

Hoods for training birds were first used in the Middle East, where they were called burkas.

Austringers are allowed to capture passage hawks, or lone, wild hawks that have left the nest and are less than a year old.

important elements of Norse mythology. The 13th-century *Poetic Edda* describes the raptors as symbols of the Norse people's combination of strength and wisdom.

As far back as 2000 B.C., people have trained birds of prey to hunt small animals such as quail, pigeons, ducks, and rabbits. This traditional sport, called falconry (using falcons) or gamehawking (using hawks or eagles), continues today. Captive birds wear a leather strap, called a jess, tied to each leg. The falconer (using falcons) or austringer (using hawks or eagles) holds the jesses between the thumb and forefinger as the bird perches on the hunter's leather-gloved hand. This is called manning the bird. The birds also wear a soft, leather hood to keep them calm. When the hunter removes the hood and lets go of the straps, the prey's slightest movement catches the bird's attention and prompts it to attack. While birds do not typically retrieve prey for their masters, they do kill it and hold it on the ground until the hunter can retrieve it. Sometimes a bird of prey is used only to flush out prey, which the hunter then shoots.

In what is today northern Iraq, **archaeologists** discovered wall art depicting falconry in the palace of the Assyrian king Sargon II, which dates to 705 B.C. By

the fourth century A.D., falconry and gamehawking had spread across Southeast Asia, and within 100 years, the sport was popularized in ancient Rome. Falconry soon became an important form of hunting in Europe and Russia. The 12th-century cleric Hugh of Fouilloy wrote a book called *De Avibus* (*The Aviarium*), in which he described the symbolism of many birds, including hawks.

The book explained that medieval monks saw the captive hawk as a symbol of their commitment to the Catholic Church. The perch represented the righteousness of religion placed high above earthly desires, and the jesses on the

143. AN UNKNOWN

June 15.—TO-DAY I noticed a new large bird, size of a nearly grown hen—a haughty, white-bodied dark-wing'd hawk—I suppose a hawk from his bill and general look— only he had a clear, loud, quite musical, sort of bell-like call, which he repeated again and again, at intervals, from a lofty dead tree-top, overhanging the water. Sat there a long time, and I on the opposite bank watching him. Then he darted down, skimming pretty close to the stream—rose slowly, a magnificent sight, and sail'd with steady wide-spread wings, no flapping at all, up and down the pond two or three times, near me, in circles in clear sight, as if for my delectation. Once he came quite close over my head; I saw plainly his hook'd bill and hard restless eyes.

excerpt from Specimen Days, *by Walt Whitman (1819–92)*

hawks' feet that held it to the perch represented the monks' ties to their religion, which are unbreakable. The custom of an austringer's carrying a hawk on the left hand is still in practice today. This comes from the medieval belief that the left hand was the bearer of material possessions, while the right hand reached for eternal and spiritual elements (such as heaven). The hawk would leave the left hand and fly to the right—as though soaring toward eternity.

Today, a hawk from New York City has become a celebrity. In the early 1990s, a pair of red-tailed hawks built a nest on a ledge of a luxury Fifth Avenue apartment building overlooking Central Park. This was one of the first urban buildings known to be used as a nesting area for red-tailed hawks, and people began following the hawks' exploits. Female hawks came and went, but the male stayed and was nicknamed "Pale Male" by birdwatchers. In 1999, Marie Winn wrote *Red-Tails in Love: A Wildlife Drama in Central Park* about Pale Male, and in 2002, Pale Male became the subject of a documentary that carried his name. Winn maintained a website of photos and news about the bird.

In the U.S., the hawk was adopted by the Studebaker Corporation to represent one of its most stylish cars.

This 14th-century carved ivory artifact shows a man holding a hawk as a deity strikes a young woman with love's arrow.

The Golden Hawk could attain 60 miles (97 km) per hour in 8 seconds and had a top speed of 130 miles (209 km) per hour.

Produced only from 1956 to 1958, the Golden Hawk is considered by many classic car enthusiasts to be the precursor to the 1960s muscle cars. Like real hawks, this powerful car had an upper body that was a different color from the lower body, and in its day, the Golden Hawk outperformed the Ford Thunderbird and the Chevrolet Corvette. Other Studebaker cars in the Hawk series of the '50s and '60s included the Flight, Power Hawk, and Sky Hawk. In 2008, the Golden Hawk was commemorated on a U.S. postage stamp as part of a five-stamp set of classic cars, and at a 2011 auction, a collector paid $99,000 for one of the cars.

Many sports teams have also chosen the hawk to represent their strength and fortitude. Indiana University of Pennsylvania changed its nickname from the Indians to the Crimson Hawks in 2007, while the Hartford Hawks' mascot, Howie the Hawk, has been a mainstay at the University of Hartford in Connecticut since the 1950s. For nearly 60 years, students at St. Joseph's University in Philadelphia have been selected to wear the red-and-brown hawk costume as the mascot for the St. Joseph's Hawks, and since 1959, students have worn the black-and-gold Herky

the Hawk costume for the University of Iowa's Hawkeyes.
The State University of New York at New Paltz has kept
a live mascot for its Hawks sports teams on campus since
1951, when Gus the goshawk was first introduced. Over
the years, female mascots named Gussie have also held
the rotating position. Hugo, a costumed mascot, cheers
on the New Paltz Hawks at games. A basketball team that
began as the Buffalo Bisons and later became the Tri-
Cities Blackhawks eventually gained fame as the National
Basketball Association's Atlanta Hawks, whose Hall-of-
Famers include sharp-eyed highfliers Connie Hawkins,
Moses Malone, and Pete Maravich.

Built at a cost of $213.5 million, Philips Arena has been home to the Atlanta Hawks since 1999.

Fossilized skeletons of
Archaeopteryx *have enabled
people to imagine what the
animal may have looked like.*

LOATHED AND LOVED

B irds **evolved** from hollow-boned reptiles that
existed millions of years ago. The link between
these two kinds of animals is possibly the
Archaeopteryx, a creature with feathered wings
and reptilian teeth. Though it died out about 65 million
years ago, other birdlike creatures continued to evolve.
Fossils indicate that the first raptors appeared about 50
million years ago. Compared with modern hawks, the
largest of which is only five pounds (2.3 kg), prehistoric
birds were enormous. First described in 1937 from fossil
remains found in a cave in the Bahamas, *Titanohierax
gloveralleni* (also known as the Bahaman titan-hawk)
weighed as much as 16 pounds (7.3 kg). A fierce hunter
of mammals, reptiles, and other birds, the titan-hawk
was one of the islands' top predators.

Scientists believe that the Ciboney Indians, the first
humans to inhabit the Bahamas, shared the islands with
titan-hawks. The Ciboney mysteriously disappeared, but
were soon replaced by Arawak Indians who arrived from
the Amazon region of South America in the 8th century
A.D. Increased human settlement disrupted the islands'

A young shikra's spotted
undersides develop into the
banded pattern typical of
adults as the bird ages.

**The shikra was
named for its
historical use in
falconry in India
and Pakistan, for
"shikra" means
"hunter" in Hindi.**

The number of migrating Swainson's hawks in Argentina is declining because of pesticide poisoning.

natural balance, and many animal species—including titan-hawks—began to disappear. Today, only sharp-shinned, white-tailed, and red-tailed hawks can be found in the Bahamas and West Indies.

While many hawk species are abundant today, some species, such as the Ridgway's hawk, are dangerously close to extinction. Although Ridgway's hawks feed almost exclusively on reptiles, farmers have long believed these birds prey on **domesticated** fowl and have hunted them relentlessly. Ridgway's hawks have been wiped out of their native Haiti, and now fewer than 120 pairs exist only in the Dominican Republic. The Gundlach's hawk, which is found only in Cuba, has also suffered persecution from farmers. This endangered bird actually does prey on poultry. Hawks also suffer from electrocution on power lines, collisions with tall buildings and objects such as wind **turbines** and radio towers, and from eating **contaminated** prey. Most hawks, though, simply die out when their habitats are destroyed.

An understanding of how humans influence hawks is vital to hawk conservation efforts. The Red-Shouldered Hawk Study is an ongoing research project involving the

first-documented population of red-shouldered hawks to
have **adapted** to life in a suburban area. Since 1997, the
Cincinnati, Ohio, study has used a process called banding
to collect data on nesting and reproduction, home
ranges, diet, and survival. Nestlings' legs are fitted with
an aluminum United States Geological Survey bracelet,
called a band, on one leg and a plastic band imprinted
with numbers and letters on the other leg. The code
on the plastic band can be read using binoculars, which
allows researchers to count and monitor the birds without
needing to recapture them. The information collected on

*Logging of hardwood forests has
led to a decline in red-shouldered
hawk populations in such habitats.*

The northern goshawk is the largest member of the "true" hawks, with females averaging nearly three pounds (1.4 kg).

the suburban red–shouldered hawks has provided a better understanding of how birds of prey can successfully adapt to habitat shared closely by humans.

A series of research projects conducted by HawkWatch International in Salt Lake City, Utah, is designed to count, track, and monitor migratory raptors. In one project, HawkWatch captures birds, bands them, and then releases them. Over periods of months and years, the birds are recaptured and identified by their bands. This method of gathering data works well to count numbers of birds, but for its study on migration and patterns of habitat use, HawkWatch must employ technology.

The HawkWatch **satellite**-tracking program follows red-tailed hawks and northern goshawks across the western U.S. and golden eagles migrating from Alaska to Mexico. Some of the questions HawkWatch researchers use to guide them are whether individual birds follow the same migration routes each year, where new birds that join migration routes originate, and how different raptor species use shared habitats. Satellite transmitters offer the best method for answering such questions. The transmitter is a **Global Positioning System** (GPS) device that is small and lightweight enough to be carried on a bird's back. About the size of a nine-volt battery, the device is situated in the middle of the bird's back between its wings.

The transmitter inside the device sends out a signal once a day. A satellite picks up the signal and sends it to a computer that maintains a map of the bird's movements. Transmitter batteries are designed to last for two years, though some of the devices include mini solar panels that use the sun's energy to extend the battery life. Since 1999, nearly 100 birds of prey have been satellite-tracked by HawkWatch. A series of maps and details about the tracked birds can be found on HawkWatch's website.

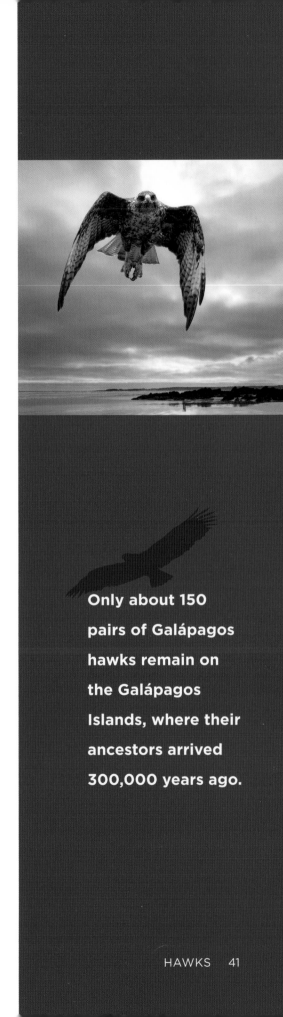

Only about 150 pairs of Galápagos hawks remain on the Galápagos Islands, where their ancestors arrived 300,000 years ago.

Most hawk species are territorial and will fiercely defend their hunting grounds against invading birds.

Many hawk species store food in a hiding spot, called a cache, near their nest for later consumption.

Home to one of the largest **captive-breeding** programs in the world, the Canadian Raptor Conservancy in Simcoe, Ontario, breeds 15 different raptor species—many endangered—each year. To help decrease the number of birds captured in the wild, the Conservancy provides captive-bred hawks for the sport of gamehawking and trains some of its birds for use in Hollywood, including 2 Harris's hawks that appeared in the movies *Jewel* and *Lost and Delirious* in 2001 and 10 different raptors that appeared on the Public Broadcasting System children's show *Zoboomafoo* from 1999 to 2001. As part of its conservation program, the Conservancy releases some of its young raptors back into their natural habitats.

Dr. Josef Schmutz, a lecturer at the University of Saskatchewan in Saskatoon, has been studying ferruginous, red-tailed, and Swainson's hawks for more than 30 years. His research has focused on the relationship between these raptors and their prairie habitat, which has been affected by the development of farm- and ranchland. Schmutz uses artificial nesting sites—platforms on tall poles—to study hawks' nesting behaviors. He also examines how agricultural practices influence hawks' prey

and, by extension, hawks' hunting and feeding behaviors.

Raptor research can lead to better land and wildlife management practices that protect the natural balance of **ecosystems**. As humans reach ever farther into wilderness areas, we must learn to live with wild animals and they with us. Hawks depend on our conservation and education efforts to help their human neighbors recognize the value of these amazing birds of prey and understand the important roles they play in the health of our planet.

Until the mid-20th century, Swainson's hawks were considered pests and routinely shot at night while they slept.

ANIMAL TALE: HAWK CARRIES THE SUN

The Congo River, the world's second-largest, flows east to west along the eastern border of the Democratic Republic of the Congo. According to this tale from the Mongo people of the region, the hawk played an important role in the origins of the world.

Long ago, when the first people lived in the world, the only light came from the moon. One night, a woman went to the river to ask the goddess of the river for a child. The river goddess took two eggs from a hawk's nest and gave them to the woman, who hurried home with them to show her husband.

For 30 days, the couple watched the eggs until, finally, out of one egg hatched a beautiful young hawk, whom they named Nkombe, and out of the other egg hatched a strong little boy, whom they named Mokele. The couple and their children were the first family in the world.

As Mokele and Nkombe grew up, their father taught them how to work hard and care for others. The hawks taught them to always have a keen eye and make quick use of their sharp hunting tools— Mokele's spear and Nkombe's talons. The brothers were curious and bold. One day, Mokele asked his father, "Why is the sky so dim?"

His father told him about Chief Mokulaka, who ruled over the Land of the Sun far to the east. "He will not share the sun with the rest of the world."

"I will go there," said Mokele. "Nkombe will go with me, and we will bring the sun here."

Mokele traveled by canoe to the Land of the Sun, and Nkombe flew by his side. The journey was long. In the Land of the Sun, Mokele asked Chief Mokulaka to share the sun with Mokele's world. "Come to my home for supper," the chief said to Mokele, "and I will give you my answer."

When Mokele and Nkombe arrived at the chief's home, the chief invited them to sit at his table, where a banquet was laid out. "This is my daughter," said the chief, "who prepared this fine meal." When the chief's daughter walked into the room, she and Mokele fell in love immediately. Suddenly, she threw herself at the table and tossed all the dishes onto the floor.

"Father," she cried, "you cannot poison them!" She ran to Mokele and took his hand.

Chief Mokulaka shook with fury at his daughter for revealing his deceptive plan to kill the intruders. "You must share the sun with his world," the daughter said, "or I will go away with him and never return."

The chief loved his daughter more than the sun, so he agreed to her demand. And as much as Mokele wished for her to become his wife, he was glad he could keep his promise to his family. To this day, Nkombe the hawk carries the sun in his strong talons each day back and forth between the Land of the Sun and the rest of the world. Nkombe brings the sun to the east each morning, and every night he carries the sun back to the west, behind the moon, to the Land of the Sun.

GLOSSARY

adapted – changed to improve its chances of survival in its environment

archaeologists – people who study human history by examining ancient peoples and their artifacts

captive-breeding – being bred and raised in a place from which escape is not possible

carrion – the rotting flesh of an animal

contaminated – negatively affected by exposure to a polluting substance

cultures – particular groups in a society that share behaviors and characteristics that are accepted as normal by that group

domesticated – tamed to be kept as a pet or used as a work animal or farm product

ecosystems – communities of organisms that live together in environments

egg tooth – a hard, toothlike tip of a young bird's beak or a young reptile's mouth, used only for breaking through its egg

evolved – gradually developed into a new form

extinction – the act or process of becoming extinct; coming to an end or dying out

Global Positioning System – a system of satellites, computers, and other electronic devices that work together to determine the location of objects or living things that carry a trackable device

metabolism – the processes that keep a body alive, including making use of food for energy

migrate – to undertake a regular, seasonal journey from one place to another and then back again

mythology – a collection of myths, or popular, traditional beliefs or stories that explain how something came to be or that are associated with a person or object

ornithologists – scientists who study birds and their lives

poachers – people who hunt protected species of wild animals, even though doing so is against the law

pupil – the dark, circular opening in the center of the eye through which light passes

satellite – a mechanical device launched into space; it may be designed to travel around Earth or toward other planets or the sun

turbines – machines that produce energy when wind or water spins through their blades, which are fitted on a wheel or rotor

warm-blooded – maintaining a relatively constant body temperature that is usually warmer than the surroundings

SELECTED BIBLIOGRAPHY

ARKive. "Red-tailed Hawk (*Buteo jamaicensis*)." http://www.arkive.org/red-tailed-hawk/buteo-jamaicensis/.

Clark, William S., and Brian K. Wheeler. *Hawks of North America*. 2nd ed. New York: Houghton Mifflin, 2001.

Dunne, Pete. *The Wind Masters: The Lives of North American Birds of Prey*. New York: Mariner Books, 2003.

HawkWatch International. "Species Fact Sheets." http://www.hawkwatch.org/about-raptors/species-fact-sheets.

Snyder, Noel, and Helen Snyder. *Raptors of North America: Natural History and Conservation*. Stillwater, Minn.: Voyageur Press, 2006.

Weidensaul, Scott. *The Raptor Almanac: A Comprehensive Guide to Eagles, Hawks, Falcons, and Vultures*. Guilford, Conn.: Lyons Press, 2004.

Note: Every effort has been made to ensure that any websites listed above were active at the time of publication. However, because of the nature of the Internet, it is impossible to guarantee that these sites will remain active indefinitely or that their contents will not be altered.

Santa Fe Island is home to a healthy population of Galápagos hawks that enjoy a protected habitat amidst *Opuntia* cactus.

INDEX